The Life of
THOMAS L. LIDGETT,

AS WRITTEN BY HIMSELF.

THE LIFE OF
THOMAS L. LIDGETT.

ONE OF LINCOLNSHIRE'S BEST KNOWN MEN.

AS WRITTEN BY HIMSELF.

The Idea of the Writer was to show there is never need for despair, but there is hope for all.

This Work has been printed as written, in the plain, straightforward, unvarnished manner in which "Tommy Lidgett" always spoke, and has not been tampered with in the slightest degree by literary critics.

LINCOLN:
PRINTED AND PUBLISHED BY W. K. MORTON & SONS, LTD., "CHRONICLE" OFFICE,
290, HIGH STREET.

INTRODUCTION.

November 11th, 1908.

This book was written by my father during the last few months of his life, to try to do people who might read it some good. His object was to give a lame dog a lift over a stile, as many people besides myself know. I noticed his failing strength most from about last June, and he knew it also, but he did not fear death in the least. On September 9th last, he was rather worried at not having corrected his writing, and I read it to him and he corrected it in the places it needed correction, and he seemed very glad to think he had at last finished it. On October 17th, 1908, the day before he died, I wrote to him telling him I was going to get it published ready for him to sell before Christmas. He received that letter of course, on Sunday, the 18th, the day he was taken from us, and my brother Charles, who was with him at Wainfleet, told me afterwards how delighted he was that at last it was to be in book form. I can only give details of his beautiful death from the description of others, which are appended below. I can only add he was a very hard worker in religious matters, and went quite his own way, and helped where he saw his help was needed. He was diligent in business, and was a man of great endurance and perseverance, a very kind and loving father. His favourite hymn was "A shelter in the time of storm." The books which he delighted to read were the Bible, "Pilgrim's Progress," and the "Life of the Rev. Parkinson Milson." He loved the hills and valleys in his native county (Lincolnshire); birds, trees and flowers had a great attraction for him. He loved to be roving from one place to another, and his great motto all his life was "Do unto a man as you would have him do to you."

Yours sincerely,

TOM LIDGETT.

DEATH OF MR. T. L. LIDGETT.

EXTRACT FROM THE LOCAL PRESS, OCT. 24TH.

Death under circumstances which some people would call tragic—though it is distinctly a matter of opinion—has taken away one of the most familiar citizens of Lincoln this week. Mr. T. L. Lidgett, jeweller, of High-street, is known to nearly everybody, and the circle of his friends is both very wide and very crowded. But he was perhaps best known in religious and particularly in evangelistic circles. Religious service was a work he loved, and to those who best understood his nature, there is triumph rather than tragedy, in the fact that he has fallen in the midst of it. So it has changed.

Mr. T. L. Lidgett had been at Wainfleet for a week conducting a sale, and as he was staying the week-end there, he was asked to address the people of Wainfleet on Sunday. At night he gave his services to the local branch of the Salvation Army. After one of the officers had offered up prayer, Mr. Lidgett again rose, and prayed at some length. Then he quietly resumed his seat, whilst the congregation joined in the hymn, "Say are you ready if the death angel should call." It is an impressive hymn. One could quite understand it would have a strong hypnotic influence upon anyone who might not be feeling very well. At any rate, it was scarcely half through when Mr. Lidgett collapsed and fell to the ground apparently lifeless. The service was stopped, and Dr. Wolfendale was immediately sent for. But earthly skill was of no avail. The death angel had called, and the worker had straightway left all and followed Him. A sad feature of the disastrous event is the fact that the same morning Mr. Lidgett received a letter from his eldest son, saying he was making arrangements for the publishing of his auto-biography, which the deceased, after years upon years of toil, had just completed. It goes without saying that the life of such a man will prove most interesting reading.

He was greatly interested in temperance work, and was always willing to render assistance to anyone who gave him the opportunity.

In business, the selling of a watch was his delight, and he took pride in the fact that he introduced the Waltham lever watch into the City of Lincoln.

About five years ago Mr. Lidgett had a very bad attack of rheumatic fever, which kept him a prisoner in the house eight months, and left him with a weak heart. He was then attended by Dr. Collier and Dr. O'Neil, who warned the family

LETTER FROM AN EYE WITNESS.

that his end might come suddenly. The day before his death he told his eldest son that he felt better than he had done for weeks, and even on the fatal day he did not complain.

Of Mr. Lidgett's character we need add very little. There was no more straight-forward and honest man living, and he gained the esteem and admiration of his audience in the market-place, as well as of the congregations which he addressed from the pulpit, principally by saying what he meant, without the slightest shuffling. His characteristic feature, however, was his generosity, which was the only characteristic in his life that was manifest under a cloak, but which was a very real and ample thing. He has given hundreds of pounds away; to whom the recipients themselves only know.

Deceased leaves a widow, three sons, and a daughter, who have received the sympathy of the whole county in their sad and sudden bereavement.

Several hundreds of people gathered at the burial service in the cemetery to see the last rites of the burial service carried out.

LETTER FROM AN EYE WITNESS.

Mount Pleasant,

Wainfleet,

21/10/08.

My Dear Mrs. Lidgett,

Begging you will pardon my boldness in taking this liberty, but I was present on Sunday night during the whole of the service at the Salvation Army; and I thought you might like to know some things your husband said during his last hour on earth. Mr. Lidgett came to my husband during the open air service, and said he had been rather unwell in the afternoon, but he felt better again, and would go inside and give a few leaflets away, and during the service he seemed bright and cheerful. He spoke about the Holy Ghost, and I never heard him speak with such power, the whole congregation sat spellbound for 45 minutes. then the officer closed in prayer, but before the people moved, Mr. Lidgett broke out in prayer again, he seemed so much in

THE LIFE OF THOMAS L. LIDGETT.

earnest about their souls, "it was a real personal talk with God," they were the last words he spoke. When I had ceased to pray, the officer started to sing:

"Say, are you ready
If the death angel should call?"

and Mr. Lidgett turned from the reading desk and placed one knee on the seat and his hands on the back for about one minute, then fell backwards, gave just two gasps as if for breath, and never spoke or moved again. It scarce seemed like dying, he went so calm. During his sermon he spoke very tenderly of his family, once he said when he wrote home to tell you he had won a soul for the Master, you would say to Flossy "Another star for dad's crown," then he said they that turn many to righteousness shall shine as the star for ever and ever, and he said it with such effect that we shall never forget. At another time he said the dear Lord had done so much for him that he loved him so, if it was not for the pain and grief it would cause his family he would like to go home just then. He said, hear me friends, I am reckoning of going to my inheritance, and he looked so very happy. Well I am afraid I shall weary you with such a long letter in concluding accept our deepest sympathy.

Yours very humbly,

MRS. PORTUS.

PREFACE.

This book was written in 1908, to show the reader he need not despair. Though he be born of poor parents, God made and cares for them as well as the rich.

In the picturesque valley of Rothwell, with a stream of splendid water running down the side of the street, commencing about a mile from the village at the foot of a large chalk hill, was where I spent the happy days of my childhood, and the last two or three years I went to school at Caistor, which was a long distance My parents lived a mile out of the village of Rothwell, making the distance to Caistor and back 7 miles a day, but my father got the blacksmith to make me an iron bowl and bowl stick which got me there and back in much less time.

I pray the following truthful pages of this book will be helpful to many.

T. L. LIDGETT.

THE LIFE OF
THOMAS L. LIDGETT.

"If there be no enemy, no fight; if no fight, no victory; if no victory,
no crown."

EARLY DAYS.

I was born at Rothwell, near Caistor, in Lincolnshire, on
the 20th December, 1844, and about the age of three and a
half years I went with my mother to Moortown Station to go
to Hull. I thought when in the train we were not moving,
but that the stacks, trees, etc., were running past us in a
desperate hurry.

At the age of five I began school, with a drab smock with
a hole at each side to put my hands through, so that I could
put them in my trouser's pockets to keep them warm.

About this time I went to Moortown Station with my
father to fetch a load of coal, and while there a passenger
train arrived, I ran to the platform to look at the engine
which was named "Prince Albert," this was the grandest
sight I had ever seen in my life, so far.

About nine years of age I began to work 'tenting' cows
in the lanes, and birds from the corn-fields at two-pence a
day. I had an old gun and some powder, but no shot, so I
used to get bits of lead anywhere I could and cut it up with
an old knife and use it for shot, and anything that came in
my way, such as water-rats, hedge-sparrows, stock-doves, etc.,
had to mind their existence was not put an end to with these
pieces of lead.

I used to go to Caistor fair at Michaelmas with twopence
for pocket money, and buy a pound of hazel pears and a
pennyworth of sweets, and then want more money, but no
more could I get.

At the age of twelve my father and mother left Rothwell
and went to live at Thoresway, and stayed there over thirty
years.

THE LIFE OF THOMAS L. LIDGETT.

I went to work now for sixpence a day with horses on the land, and among sheep in winter. At sixteen years of age I went to live with a farmer in Thoresway Parish named Surfleet. I soon found out I had left home when I had left my mother's fireside. I was very unsettled for weeks, but did not let outsiders know this, but my mind was often away on the ocean, or with an engine, or in some foreign land.

During this year of service I had some wonderful strivings of the good spirit of God, that wanted to lead me to a better life, but I had no one that came near enough to point me to the Lamb of God that taketh away the sins of the world.

When I received my wages at May Day, £4 5s. 0d., in 1861, I got a few clothes, etc., and £2 I paid for an old verge watch, and got a situation to live with John W. Dawber, of Beasby, on that beautiful Wold hill top where your eyes could feast on the splendid scenery of the marsh country from Grimsby to Somercotes, and the rolling sea beyond. I was more settled here, my foreman, Joseph Parsons, was as good as a father to me.

During this year I went to the Primitive Methodist Chapel at Wold Newton, and became a member with my foreman, but in an evil hour I slipped and stumbled, and fell from my humble, but happy position, and great was the fall for me. I became uneasy at times, very desponding, my trouble I kept to myself instead of taking it to Jesus at once; and I fear this is the reason we have so many backsliders to-day, they listen to the laughs and scorns of a deceitful world, and a wideawake devil who has been saturated with deceit thousands of years, and is too cunning for any poor sin stricken son of any mother to listen to.

In this situation I stayed till May 14th, 1864, but my mind never settled, I had got a load of guilt to carry, I had left my best friend "Jesus," and was now walking on the downward track which some people call "broad and easy," but I found it hard work going down to destruction with a load of sin to carry.

Time kept moving onward, and the sea in the distance about ten miles had great attraction for me, the steamers with their long trails of smoke behind, and the sailing ships with their sails set, going and coming, made me wish I was a sailor.

In the commencement of 1864, I had my first sweetheart, who was housemaid to my master, whose name was Mary, and I was tempted to go to see Mary occasionally when my day's work was done; but one night I heard Mrs. Dawber in the kitchen, when I went up to the back door and I stepped across the yard and went into the coal house, but she saw the door close, and came to open it, but I was holding fast by the handle inside, when she fetched the cook to help her, then Mary to help to open the door, then I heard an order given for Mary to fetch the master out of the garden, so I came out of my hiding place and went home. After I had been in bed a few minutes the groom came for the foreman to see the master about this lad (Tom) being in the coal-house but the foreman smoothed things down and all went well till I left, May 14th, 1864.

It was now April, and I resolved that I would no longer be a farmer's servant, though I had been well treated. I stayed till my time was up and left; spent May-day week same as other lads, then went to Grimsby to seek work. After searching several days I got work to go to Barnoldby-le-Beck, to help to repair some old houses for about a month, then I went home without having any more work to do, but the clergyman at Thoresway gave me work for a month in his garden and paid me on Saturday night, and I was once again without work. I paid my mother for board and lodgings, and on the following Monday morning mother got up at 1.30, made me some coffee, so I had my last breakfast I intended having in the home at Thoresway, before I got work.

I left at five o'clock on a splendid summer morning, my mother went to the garden gate with me, gave me a kiss and a half-penny and told me to keep it till I had no other money in the world and was hungry, then buy a half-penny cake.

(I am now sixty-three years of age, and still I hold the half-penny, "my mother's gift"). I had eleven or twelve miles to walk to Grimsby, with a small bundle of shirts and stockings to carry, and my home though poor, was left behind. I was by myself all the way, wondering how things would turn out. I remembered also my sweetheart, Mary, who had gone several miles away to a situation.

I got work at Grimsby docks the same day that I left home; which was unloading steamers and sometimes carrying timber till my hands were so sore I could not close them.

One fine morning, when I had nothing to do, I stood on the dry dock gates leaning over the rail, and a man named John Brusey, a smack owner, came by and asked me if I wanted anything to do, I replied, "Yes," he said he wanted such a one as me to go to sea in his smack. I told him I would go. He seemed rather surprised at my quick answer, and showed me the vessel named "Fidelity." I was dressed in my farming suit, "white slop, red plush waistcoat, corduroy trousers, calico shirt, red cotton handkerchief and a billy-cock hat." Reader just fancy a country Joskin" going to sea like that.

I went and hung my old watch in my bedroom at my lodgings in Grimsby, gave orders if I never came back, and any of my friends ever came to enquire about me, they were to have the watch.

The dock gates were opened, and among other vessels the "Fidelity" was steered out into the Humber with this farmer's lad on board as "cook" for the crew. It was a splendid morning and the vessel went gaily with the tide down the river. I could see trees and other objects on the top of the wold hills, where I had ploughed, and said some day I would be a sailor. I had feasted my stomach with a pound of plums before going on board, and now the sailors brought some hard biscuits and fat pork out for lunch. I had some with the others, but very soon the plums and pork began to ferment in my stomach, and I was very glad to get to the side of the vessel and part with all I had, and throw it into the sea. I had looked from Beasby top at this river Humber many times with a belief that I should find happiness as a sailor, but now I was so ill I had to lay down anywhere, I could neither work nor eat, but I thought about parting with mother, and I also remembered Mary, but each day brought me further out at sea, and a greater distance between me and all my friends on shore.

After I recovered from my sea-sickness I was expected to do the work of the cook of the "Fidelity." I was ordered one morning to get some salt beef out of a cask in the hold, and also prepare the potatoes and put them in a pot for dinner. When this was done, and the pot on the fire, I went down in the hold for some water, and on coming up again the skipper said, "Farmer, where did you put the dinner?" I answered, "In the pot on the fire, sir." "Just go down in the cabin," said the skipper, "and see where they are now," and to my surprise, pot and dinner was on the cabin floor. I had not lashed the pot on the fire, and with a stiff breeze and a heavy rolling sea, which made the "Fidelity" rear up like a jibbing horse, caused this mess with the dinner.

The fishing part of the voyage I had not much to do with, only to help to heave the net up and attend to the fishermen. My bed was a wooden locker, and my pillow an oil frock belonging one of my shipmates. I was never washed from leaving Grimsby till I returned.

My skipper asked me one night to read the "testament" to him, which came home like daggers to my aching heart; for instead of the happiness I was seeking, I was finding the lash was coming hard across me. I had left the Saviour and home, and the little Primitive Methodist Chapel at Wold Newton, where I had been a member, and all these things seemed to say:

"What peaceful hours I once enjoyed,
How sweet their memory still,
But they have left an aching void,
The world can never fill."

The sea even to-day has very great charms for me, but it does not bring that peace which a backslider needs.

After a few days, our vessel was turned round for home, and that made me glad, as I was tired of this first voyage. One morning at six o'clock we arrived in Grimsby dock, with this, once a clean farmer's boy with his white slop, now more like a chimney sweep. The owner was there and asked me how I liked it, I said, "Very well sir," he says "You will go again farmer?" "No sir, I never shall," said I. After the fish was taken out of the vessel, which we had fetched from the bottom of the "deep blue sea," I was paid a few shillings, and **very** glad I was to go to my lodgings and wash the dirt of a sea voyage from my skin.

I very soon got work again on the docks, and shortly after I was a number taker on the coal drop at Grimsby, shipping coals. For five and a half years I stayed there, then this unsettled state of mind came over me again, and **I was** asked by a travelling auctioneer named Rees, if I would travel with him; I decided quickly I would, so I left the railway in eight hours' notice, and went with him.

On leaving Grimsby a young woman gave me a **new** Bible to read, and after a few months I had a letter from her, asking if I had read the book she gave me, and I don't know that I had ever looked inside it, but I resolved to read it all, and I did so in eight months, then I wrote and told her I had read the book through. I found words that I had read, and had been encouraged by years before, were making my conscience smart very keenly, yet I was still seeking happiness in my own way, and made a resolution that I would go abroad; but I never carried that resolution out, there always was my mother, whom I loved, and from whom I could not go far away, to injure her true motherly feelings.

THE MAN WITH THE HARDWARE VAN.

(I wrote these few lines to her whilst with an Auctioneer's Van belonging to a man named Rees, in the year 1870).

Here comes the chap from the Hardware Van
   That you all love so dear,
He's trying to do the best he can,
   Without the aid of beer.

He never drinks the liquors strong,
   Which ruins many a man,
But he's happy as he travels along,
   With Rees and his hardware van.

He loves you all at Thoresway Grange,
   And he knows you love him too,
Though far away from you he may range,
   He'll always think of you.

EARLY DAYS.

Though nine there be in our family,
  I hope we shall all meet again,
There is one that we should love to see,
  Far across the watery main.

So good night my father and mother dear,
  My sisters and brother too,
As through the country I do steer,
  I'll always think of you.

I resolved that another change should take place in my
life, so I left the Auction Van in the City of York, in February, 1871, and came home to see my friends and dear old
Grimsby once more. I had then no idea of ever getting into
any business, but was told by a friend named McSheen to do
something for myself, so I had £24, and made a start with a
harden bag and some knives and razors, etc., to go on the
docks to sell. I sold several articles to the men with whom
I went to sea in the "Fidelity." I then got a small shop in
Kent Street, Grimsby, then I shifted to another one in Freeman Street, but in a few months finding shop keeping nothing in my line, I gave the shop up, got an auction licence,
sold my goods on the green grass (now Freeman Street
Market, Grimsby), and went to Gainsborough and got on well
in my small way of business.

The first auction room I had was a schoolroom in Becky
Lane (now Etherington Street). I began to make money
and friends, and got customers, by always giving good value
for money.

I stayed here two or three months, and then went back to
the Odd Fellows' Hall, Grimsby, for several months; I rigged
a poor platform up, not having money enough to do everything up to the mark. My run out platform was made
chiefly of orange boxes, which sometimes fell down two or
three times a night. Trade was very good and prosperity
seemed as though it was going to be a continued thing.

I then came to Lincoln and took the auction room in
Butchery Street, but when I had been here about a month,
myself and my brother were both taken very suddenly ill of
scarlet fever, which laid me up six months. My brother got
home to Thoresway, but I was too ill to be moved from

THE LIFE OF THOMAS L. LIDGETT.

Lincoln for six weeks. An Auctioneer was hired by my friends, and sold my goods for very little, till I was nearly where I started; but my pluck was good, so I came to start where I left off in Lincoln, and quickly pulled myself together again. In the year 1873, I took a trip to Scotland, and I composed in a field at Thoresway the following verses after I returned home.

TOM LIDGETT'S TRIP TO GLASGOW.

At nine in the morning, the 3rd day of June,
All nature looked gay, and flowers in bloom;
From Grimsby I started to take a long ride,
To enjoy the fresh air through the country so wide.

I started for Glasgow in Scotland to see,
For that was the town where I wanted to be;
The train was in motion very soon after nine,
And away we did go on the Manchester line.

The carriages were fastened to the engine so staunch,
We turned off at Barnetby for the Keadby branch;
We rattled along across moor and fen,
And arrived at Keadby, twenty minutes past ten.

A few minutes there and away we did range,
'Till we arrived at Doncaster, where I had to change;
The train didn't leave till five minutes to one,
So I went to the race-course, and the time was soon gone.

There was fashion and pride, and lots of fine dress,
All hast'ning away to the Northern Express;
I made one among them, not feeling proud,
But I car'd not a toss for one in the crowd.

A whistle, a cough, and the signal was given,
Then miles through the country very soon I was driven;
We arrived at Selby thirty minutes past one,
Stayed a minute or two, then proceeded along.

The City of York was the next I did see,
With its beautiful minster and high towers three;
I left there for Thirsk, fifty minutes past two,
And away to the North like the wind we did go.

TRIP TO GLASGOW.

With driver and stoker, and lots of steam power,
We arrived at Darlington five minutes to four;
Durham was the next where we stayed on the line,
Then off we did go to Newcastle-on-Tyne.

I rambled about three-quarters of an hour,
Then away I did go on my first Scottish tour;
Morpeth, Bilton, and Belford we went at full speed,
Then next we arrived at Berwick-on-Tweed.

To the far end of England I now had got stray'd,
One hundred miles further my fare I had paid;
'Twas thirty minutes past seven, the evening was fine,
When I left Old England on the North British line.

The engine was swift, and the line was straight;
We arrived at Dunbar at a quarter-past eight.
Edinboro' was next—that famous old city,—
The gas was now lighted and all things look'd pretty.

At ten minutes past nine, I bid this place adieu,
Above 40 miles further I now had to go;
We went at full speed along the Scotch glen,
And arrived at Glasgow thirty minutes past ten.

This statement is true of my ride in the train,
But I'll give you a sketch of my returning again;
I hope you'll excuse all the errors I've penned,
It was made by Tom Lidgett, the Working-man's Friend.

THE RETURN.

I sailed away from Glasgow one fine afternoon,
In a steamer called "Penguin," with steerage and saloon;
The bell rang for starting at a quarter-past three,
Friends were now parting by the side of the quay.

Some said farewell, and some good-bye, while others wav'd
    the hand,
As the ship moved gently out of sight, down the river
    Clyde so grand.
We sailed to Greenock and there stayed three hours for
    the mail,
And at 8.15 the bell did ring for England to set sail.

B

THE LIFE OF THOMAS L. LIDGETT.

Some spent the night upon the deck, and others down below
And some drank whisky freely, and were rolling to and fro;
The water was smooth and still, dispute me if you can,
At six o'clock in the morning I saw the Isle of Man.

Eight hours more we sail'd along, then England we did see,
And arriv'd all safe in Liverpool at twenty-five to three,
With the express train to Manchester I then did quickly fly,
Expecting soon to see my friends—to the Scotch I'd bid
      good-bye.

My journey it was getting short, fresh sights I now had
      seen,
In the smoky town of Sheffield I arrived at 6.15.
Then away we went to Retford, the evening it was fine,
I arrived once more in Grimsby town a little after nine.

My Scottish ramble now is past, my rhyming at an end,
But bear in mind the truth you'll find in these few lines
      I've penned,
I wish you all good health and strength as through this
      world you roam,
May you and I, when we come to die, go to a brighter home

        T. L. LIDGETT, 201, High Street, Lincoln.

After a few more months went by, I married the young
woman who gave me the Bible, when I went away from
Grimsby with the Auction Van. After our wedding, we
went to sell for ten weeks in Great Yarmouth, then we came
to Butchery Street, Lincoln, and stayed five months, and did
a splendid business. I then went to Grimsby and got a home
fitted up, No. 24, King Edward Street.

I was steady and worked hard for a few years, and God
prospered me wonderfully; I know He is kind to the sinner,
but the sins of a backslider's heart makes him so dark, that
it is like the darkness in the Land of Egypt, can be felt.

In the month of August 1879, I was robbed of about
£400 worth of watches and jewellery.

ROBBERY.

(Extract from "Lincolnshire Chronicle," August 29th, 1879.)

A daring robbery was reported to the police on Monday morning. For some time Mr. Thomas Lidgett, of Grimsby, has made occasional visits to Lincoln with a miscellaneous store of goods, which he has offered for sale by auction for an hour or two each evening in the City Auction Rooms, Butchery Street.

On Saturday evening a sale was held and continued until a quarter to eleven. Amongst the articles offered were watches, guards, rings, &c., and a large number were exposed to view. These, it would appear, excited the cupidity of some individual, for when Mr. Lidgett's assistant opened the store at 7.30 on Monday morning, the entire stock was found to have been carried off.

So far as we can gather 157 watches are missing, and a large number of wedding and keeper rings, gold and silver Albert guards, gold pins, brooches, lockets, and other trinkets, valued altogether by the proprietor at £400. The supposition is that the thief or thieves concealed themselves amongst the butchers' stalls, whilst the sale was over and the place locked up.

They then picked the lock of the side door into the Auction Rooms (which was found to be unlocked on Monday morning though secure on Saturday evening), and then quietly helped themselves to what they pleased.

The door leading into Butchery Passage and from thence into Silver Street, was locked as usual by the official living on the premises.

The thieves made an attempt to force out a staple from this door, but were unsuccessful, and then filed away the one holding the lock to the door post. This being effected, the passage would afford a very convenient means of exit, and the robbery may have been committed within a few minutes of the place being closed on Saturday evening, and whilst a large number of persons would be passing to and fro in Silver Street. If so, no suspicion would attach to anyone seen coming loaded out of the passage.

(19)

THE LIFE OF THOMAS L. LIDGETT.

(Extract from "Lincolnshire Chronicle," April 9th, 1880.)

Mr. T. L. Lidgett, of Butchery Street Auction-room, has supplied us with the following list of goods which he has recovered of the large quantity stolen from his room in August last, by a young man who was convicted of the offence at the City Quarter Sessions on Saturday last, and sentenced to 18 calendar months' imprisonment:—93 silver watches, 36 gold watches, 6 aluminum watches, 1 gold albert, 1 gold guard, 3 gold necklets, 23 gold lockets, 12 wedding rings, 9 gold keepers. 3 sets gold brooches and ear-rings, 7 pairs gold solitaires, 19 sets gold studs, 21 gold pins, 9 silver alberts, 10 silver necklets, 12 silver lockets, 11 silver brooches, 5 silver pendants, 9 silver pins, 38 plated pins, 1 plated seal, 27 plated brooches, 108 steel Alberts.

I met in Class, went to Chapel, always had a desire to be good, but evil was always present with me. I got to drinking beer and whiskey, mixed port wine and brandy together and smoked too many cigars and too much tobacco.

I went to markets and got amongst company, until the good influence seemed to be something of the past, but God never left the backslider (Tommy Lidgett). He prospered and blessed me till I had three shops in Dolphin Lane, Boston, a grocer's shop at Cleethorpes, two houses in Grimsby and a shop and auction room in Lincoln. I fastened these places of business for five years, and a few months before the lease was up I had a letter to say my mother was very ill. I went to Thoresway about February, 1889, and found my mother both very ill and dark about her soul and salvation.

I came to Lincoln, stayed a few days, I was so unsettled, that I went to Thoresway again to see my mother and she told me, Jesus Christ had forgiven all her sins, and she was only waiting for Him to call her Home. She died in the August following, and said, "I am going to be with Jesus," she was delighted to die.

A few weeks after, instead of me retiring with plenty of money, my lease was concluded, and I was not worth a shilling.

From the first giving way to sin, up to this time, "I knew the way of transgressors was hard." I was so distracted I could neither eat nor sleep, and as life seemed to be a blank, I thoroughly made up my mind to destroy myself.

ROBBERY.

I went to Grimsby, boarded on a steamer, went 800 miles to the north, intending to jump overboard; the captain was a friend of mine, and when we got to the Orkney Islands, we went on shore and he told an old man called "Jimmy," that I was very down-hearted, and Jimmy took me to his home and asked me to kneel by the side of a sofa, and Jimmy knelt by my side, and prayed earnestly that God would save me. I went on board, and went north two or three hundred miles, between the Faroe Islands and Iceland; the weather became heavy and the sailors fastened a rope from stem to stern, that they might seize it when the heavy waves rolled over the ship, to save them being washed overboard. I was prompted to go forward and take hold of this rope, and when the big waves came up, was tempted to leave go and so be washed away; but God in his mercy prevented me leaving go of the rope.

I wrote the following lines a year or two after the fishing trip:—

T. L. LIDGETT'S 14 DAYS VOYAGE ON A FISHING STEAMER TO THE FAROE ISLANDS.

Before I begin my narrative, I will explain to you where the Faroe Islands are situated. They lay 230 miles north of Scotland, about 180 miles south-east of Iceland; they are in the North Atlantic Ocean, 7 degrees west of the meridian of Greenwich.

On the 7th of July, 1891, at 6 o'clock in the morning, I took my stand beside Captain Wadmore, on the bridge of the steamship "Doric," in Grimsby Fish Dock. I stood watching the shore as we steamed down the Humber, and after passing Cleethorpes we rounded Spurn Point, and then we were in the open sea. After we passed Scarborough and other places on the coast, we steamed due north. The next place of note I saw was Aberdeen, the Scotch granite city. Then Peterhead, the centre of the northern whalers. Then we passed Wick, the centre of the herring fishery. I saw John O'Groats, which is in the county of Caithness, in the north of Scotland. It was a dismal sight, the weather was changed, and a choppy sea, and tons of water washing over the deck. But away we went night and day, till we arrived at Stromness, in the Orkney Islands, where we put in and purchased £5 worth of fresh herrings, for bait for our fishing expedition. Then we steamed away for another 200 miles further north, until we reached the Faroe Islands, which belong to the Danes. The houses I saw were built of wood, the grass is like moss, and the sheep are very small, and not unlike foxes at a distance. In the morning we steamed out of the bay, where we had laid all night, and began our luck for fish. We had now got within 180 miles of Iceland, where the sun never sets for three months in the year. There are many thousands of birds of various sizes in this part; they build their nests on the ledges of rocks on the Faroe Islands, and fly to Iceland every morning, 180 miles, for food for the young birds, and fly back at night. The laying down of the line for fishing commences about 5.30 in the morning, and takes from $1\frac{1}{2}$ to 2 hours, steaming gently. The line is 7 miles long, with a galvanised buoy float every mile. The buoy has a flag-staff through it, with an anchor, which goes to the bottom of the sea, and a flag at the top of the staff, so that the line can be found if it breaks. The sea in this part is 700 feet deep, or more than twice as high as Lincoln Cathedral. A short line and hook is attached every three or four yards to the main line, with part of a herring on the hook for bait. After the line is down, the crew get their breakfast, smoke their tobacco, play at cards, and tell their sea yarns, and talk a deal of home, and their frolics on shore. About 9.30 they start to draw in the line, which brings up from the deep sea the kinds of fish we daily see in our fish shops; cod fish, ling, halibut, skate, and other large fish, from 1 stone to 10 stone each. Some are eaten up by the sharks, and only the head remains on the hook. When they dress the fish on deck, the sea gull, which is often seen in our fields, are round the vessel by dozens, for bits of liver which are thrown overboard. It takes about 8 hours to draw in the line each day. After six days of this kind of work, the head of the steamer is turned south and comes full speed home with her cargo. On the way from the Faroe Islands to Aberdeen, there are many thousands of birds to be seen, from the size of a water-hen to an

TRIP TO FAROE ISLANDS.

English Swan. The fishermen have a bit of rest for about 2 days, then they begin to wash and clean, and make the steamer look trim and neat for entering the harbour at Grimsby, which is reached in 4 days and nights, full speed ahead.

This is a true account of a 14 days' voyage on a fishing steamer to the Faroe Islands.

T. L. LIDGETT.

I was put on shore at Scarboro'. I then wrote to Dr. O'Neil and asked him to meet me at the station by a certain train, but he sent a detective, who met me and asked me where I was going, and I told him I didn't know, and he said, "Let me carry your bag, and have a walk with me." I did, and he walked me to the Police Station, and got a cab and took me to Bracebridge Asylum. I was in deep distress, my will power had left me, and I had a determination to destroy my life.

I was in the asylum three months then came home for a month on trial, I got money enough to buy two bottles of brandy and stole away from my family (I bought the brandy at the "Blue Anchor"). I went a mile to a plantation, drank two bottles of brandy, pulled my coat off and rolled it up for a pillow and laid me down and said, "I shall be in hell to-morrow," this was in February, 1892. I had procured a razor, and I awoke in the morning about 4.30. I was staggering drunk, but I went to a field against a stack, took the razor out of my pocket, took my collar off, and cut a severe gash in my throat. I walked home in that miserable state, two doctors were fetched ; they would have nothing to do with me. I was put in a cab, taken to the Hospital, and they stitched my wound up with silver wire. I was three weeks in bed, then taken before the magistrates and was announced once more for the asylum, and was there fifteen months. A few labouring men took a private room in a street in Lincoln, and there met one night a week (at the time I was in the asylum), and prayed earnestly in real faith that God would restore me, and by His goodness and mercy I am living to-day.

THE LIFE OF THOMAS L. LIDGETT.

I got home through the prayers of the people, and I shall always remember that the prayers of the poor are heard in Heaven.

After I had been home a few days I had a fit of despondency, I got enough poison to kill four men, I got a bicycle and rode five miles to a woodside in a valley, on a splendid summer evening. I laid my bicycle on the green grass, and Satan seemed to stand alongside of me, urging me to destruction. I drank the 4ozs. of poison, I laid down again by the side of my bicycle with my watch in my hand, and I said, "I shall be in hell in twenty minutes," but the poison never affected me. I got up, rode home, awfully put out because I was not dead. Satan seemed to loose his grip, and the Lord's spirit worked in me.

I went to Sleaford market, and did a good business in watches, the people were delighted to see me once more, then I went to Metheringham and sold in the Club Room at the "Star and Garter" Hotel. Next morning I walked to Dunston Station, and on the way a man caught me up, who knew me, and said, " I am pleased to see you Tom, by what I have heard, I thought I should never see you again." I said, "It wouldn't have mattered," but he said, "It *would* have mattered, you would have been a lost man if you had died in the state you were in." We walked together a few yards, and he said, "I must leave you here, I am going to take a young horse a feed of corn," he shook hands with me, and said several times over, "God bless you, Tom."

I walked a hundred yards to the Railway Bridge, between Metheringham and Dunston, I stood on the bridge and looked across to the Wold Hills, then I turned round and looked towards Dunston Pillar, and I couldn't think what was the matter with me and said, "everything I see is mine." I remembered everything was not mine, but I said it is my Father's; I will trust Him, and the burden rolled away, and I gave my heart to Him and I was free. I came home and told my wife I had found Him. She said, "Who," and I said, "The Saviour." He has pardoned all my transgressions this morning and I am so happy I cannot stand still, and I yearned to tell the world the love of God to me.

TEMPTATION AND FALL.

I got a bill out for the sale at Branston, and I had scores of labouring men who came there, who knew part of my distresses, instead of selling, the first half hour I talked to them about Eternal life, and now I am sixty-three years old, and I have talked ever since about the love of God to me.

I had an impulse on the Sunday following, that I was to go and give a lecture, near Sleaford, and I replied in a blunt way to myself, and laughed and said, " I'm not having any." On Monday morning I went to Sleaford Market and the impulse grew stronger than ever, and there was a good old Wesleyan brother in the crowd at my sale, it was his dinner time. I moved for him to come to me. I left my sale and asked the man how a certain lady was getting on whose husband was killed on the railway, her circumstances were favourable, and I said, " I have to help somebody in more need." When I turned to my stall, a working man stopped me and said, "Can I speak to you," and I said "Yes," and he said to me, "We had a committee meeting yesterday afternoon at our school, and we all felt we ought to ask you to give us a lecture. Our scholars want prizes for Christmas, and we are £2 short." I told him I was not a lecturer. I asked him at what time he had that impression of me, and he said, "Just after school yesterday afternoon"; I told him I had had the same impression, and therefore I would go. I took his address, and told him I would write him what night I would come, and subject of lecture.

I sent him a subject, "A dark night on a Lincoln Common," he met me at Ruskington Station, and took me to the Wesleyan Chapel, North Kyme. The Chapel was crowded with people, and I had no lecture ready. I thought I was going to talk half an hour to a lot of labouring men, who had been at plough and other farm duties. The chairman was Mr. Willows, of Billinghay, and while they were singing the first hymn I whispered to him asking if they had prayers at these meetings, and he said "Yes," and I said, "I cannot pray and I have no lecture ready, and this great congregation of well dressed people staggers me;" but he offered up a prayer and I knelt down against a stool and prayed silently to God, and asked Him to give me words for *one hour,* and when the chairman introduced me to the people, I came to the front and could not speak, but when I opened my mouth I said, "Take me as I am, I have nothing ready," and as the spirit helped me, I spoke, and when I had gone on a few minutes I was so full with the Holy Ghost that I burned with fire. I pulled my coat off and threw it down, and I spoke *sixty-five minutes,* and at the close the collection realized £2 8s., the Lord gave me five minutes longer than the hour to talk to the people, and eight shillings more than they required.

I have never to this day been out of a job. I have never charged anybody a penny for expenses, I could not do it, after what the Lord has done for me, and I've set my face for Christ. I am going to wear out, not to rust out. I cannot loiter my time away, the fields are black with sin, and souls are dying to be saved, and its the duty of the converted to help them to be saved.

I will now give you a few instances how God has led me: One morning I got up at four o'clock (when I lived near the Stonebow). I wrote letters about my trade until five, and I was so happy I could not be still; I longed to do somebody good. I worked in my shop that morning until half-past six, and had a direct order from the Lord to me, that I was to go and buy a shoulder of mutton and take it to a certain number in a certain street. I did so, and after getting one of the young men to make it into a parcel, I then went to the house, knocked at the door, and a white-haired lady came, and I said, "I have brought a parcel," and she said "Come in!" but I would not go in, I gave her the parcel and said, "Good morning," and left.

A year and a half after I saw that lady again, and she told me that at the time I took her the mutton, her husband (who worked in the foundry), was very ill in bed, and had been in bed eleven weeks, and she said about two minutes before I had knocked at the door, with the mutton, she had just then got up from her knees, asking the Lord to send her something to eat, for they had nothing, and she said, then you came with your parcel.

LED BY THE SPIRIT OF GOD.

A few weeks after that, I took one of my men and a dray load of goods nine miles from Lincoln, and sold near a public house. After the sale my man drove home, I stayed all night, and when the house was closed, I went in to go to bed, and I saw the landlord was drinking beer in the bar by himself. It took all the strength I had to speak to him, but I felt I must do it. I looked at him and asked him if ever he prayed, and he said "I do," and I said, "I am glad you pray." I said "I pray also. I was once one of the most miserable men in the world, I prayed and the Lord heard me, and answered my prayers, and I am now one of the happiest men in this country." I also had an impulse to say to him, "Don't cease to pray, something seems to tell me you won't live long." And the man turned white, and said, "What?" "Don't cease to pray," said I, "Something seems to tell me you won't live long, and whatever you do, believe what you pray for." I went that way a short time after with my horse and trap, for an afternoon's driving. I called at the house, and the man was dead and buried. I did not know until I got there; I was very pleased I had said the words I had previously said to him.

Another man used to curse and swear, and called me awfully at Mablethorpe, while selling there in the summer nights. He used to get drunk and then come to me and annoy me many a time. Two or three years afterwards, I went to Mablethorpe, and was told he was dying; I went and bought some bananas, grapes, oranges, etc., and went across some fields to see him. When I knocked at the door, his wife said he was in the next room, in bed. I went to him and said, "Jack, are you dying," and he said "Yes." I then said "Perhaps you could eat some of these nice things?" and he looked into the bag and he said "I can," and I said "Shall we have a prayer meeting, Jack?" and he said "Yes," and we had one, and it was one of the happiest times I had experienced so far. He died shortly after, one of the most glorious deaths known at Mablethorpe.

THE LIFE OF THOMAS L. LIDGETT.

AT MABLETHORPE, SUMMER OF 1902.

I was standing on the sea shore
  With some Sheffield goods to sell;
Opposite was a sweet stall,
  And a waitress "Mountain Nell."

Bananas she was handing out
  To the poor man and the swell;
And the children playing round about
  Would buy of "Mountain Nell."

Her hair hung on her shoulders
  As she the wares did sell;
She did as her father told her,
  This sea-side "Mountain Nell."

Her brother Charlie by her side
  In fine weather and in storms,
Was selling too, close by the tide,
  To the people on the forms.
Their dad looked like the skipper
  Of a ship that sails to sea;
With ice cream he cooled the tripper
  Before they went to tea.

God bless this dear old skipper,
  While the ocean keeps its swell;
Though his life be sweet or bitter,
  May he love his "Mountain Nell."

And when the light of life is o'er,
  And his bosom cease to swell,
May he meet on a far and brighter shore
  The man who rang the bell.

                    T. L. LIDGETT, Lincoln.

It might be mentioned here, I used to ring a bell sometimes to call people up to my sale. I am the man who rang the bell.

Walking up Lincoln street one day, near the High Bridge, I had another impulse, that I was to take my horse and trap in the country, and take my daughter, and she was to drive the horse, and when we got near the Stonebow, my daughter said, "Which way am I to drive, Dad?" I told her through the Stonebow. "Then where?" she said. We will go up Silver Street and drive east a few miles, we drove to a village, and I told her to drive up to the large house, which I had pointed out to her, as I felt that was the house I was to call. When we arrived, the owner stood in the back yard, with his hands in his pockets, and said, "Are you going to stop here?" and I said, "I don't know." I asked him if he had a stable, and he said he had, so he led the horse into the yard, and his wife and daughter took my daughter into a flower garden. We put the horse into the stable, and then went into the kitchen garden and I sat down on a seat, and said to the man, "I don't know what I've come for, but I'll ask you one question. Tell me how you are getting on in the world, in every way?" and he said, "Every hour that I am in bed I am planning to destroy my life, and every hour I am out of bed, I am looking for the best place to do it. I have four ways, the engine, the river, the razor and poison." I told him I had been in that state, and added, "But it will not pay. Your wife, daughter, and your other children will mourn your loss as long as they live; the gaping world will laugh and call you a fool, and your soul will be in Hell." And he said, "I know it," and I said, "Take my advice, when I have gone out of your yard, get into a secret place, quite alone, and pour out your complaint and trouble to God, in mighty faith, and he will bring you safely through." Three months after, he walked to Lincoln, and came into my shop and clapped me on the back and said, "You're a good 'un, Tom," and I said, "There is no goodness in me," and a second time he said, "You're a good 'un, Tom." He said I will tell you something the world doesn't know. When you and your daughter came to me at the back end of the year, when I stood with my hands in my pockets, I had already fixed a rope to a beam in a loft, and a few minutes more I should have been dead. I said, "The Lord knew the time I should be there," and I said, "How did you do, after I had left you?" and he said, "I did as you said. I went into a place near where the rope was hanging, and poured out my complaint to the Lord, and he delivered me, and now I am happy"; and to-day he is one of my best friends in Lincoln. He lives retired.

THE LIFE OF THOMAS L. LIDGETT.

In January, 1906, I went into a secret place in Lincoln to pray, and I prayed to the Lord that he would send me somewhere where there was a backslider wanted saving, and in a very short space of time I had an impulse to go sixty miles in an express train. I was there about one hour and ten minutes, and took a place in which to sell for eight days. I came home to get ready, and had an impulse to take it eleven days. I did so, and when I got there to sell, something seemed to tell me to take it twenty, and on the nineteenth night I gave an address for twenty-five minutes, for the farewell to these people. When I had done I was so full of glorious liberty, I could not go on selling my goods, when a man came up and asked me if I would shake hands with him, and I said, "I don't know you, but that doesn't matter." He said, "Will you come aside, I want to tell you something privately." I went and stood with him and he said "The Lord sent you here," and I said, "How do you know?" and he said "Oh! I do know." I said "Are you a backslider?" "I have been" he said, "Yes, for six years, but was converted whilst you were giving that address, and I am now very happy, and am pleased you ever came this way." On the Sunday following, he told the people in the Railway Mission, he had been converted at an auctioneer's sale.

There are two other instances I should like to mention:— When I left Portland Place Chapel at twelve o'clock one Sunday, I came home and had my dinner, and I told my wife I had an impulse to go to a certain street in Lincoln to ask an old lady, what she thought of Eternal life. She handed me a chair, I sat down and looked at her and said, "What do you think of Eternal life?" she held both her hands up and said, "I am seventy-nine, and nobody has asked me such a thing in my life," and I said "The Lord has sent me." "You can have it without money," the old lady cried, and when I was going away, she asked me to stay longer, and I said, "Remember, what I told you. I won't tell you any more to-day." I sent her the Primitive Hymn Book, I used to write her letters in the early morning, I took her out in my trap for drives, and in three years she was taken ill for death.

LED BY THE SPIRIT OF GOD.

I had been away a week, and when I came home I went to see her. When I went to her bedside she said, "You've been a long while, I wanted you to help me to sing." I said, "What did you want me to sing?" she said, "Jesu, Lover of my Soul." I said, "Do you know Him." She said "Yes, He has been to my house and saved me, and I'm ready to go." She died very happy and went to glory.

A publican, nine miles out of Lincoln, was taken ill. I heard tell of it, so I went to see him, to tell him I had brought a message from God that he could be saved in an "Ale House," and go straight to Heaven. I took him fruit and other things suitable for a sick person, and went to see him once a week from October to February. A month before he died, I said to one of my men, "I will make a special journey to see that dying Publican. I am going to ask him one question, which I know now, he will answer. I am going to ask him if he is afraid of death." When I got to his bedside I asked him and he said, "No, I'm not afraid of death. He has forgiven me and pardoned my sins in this Ale House, and I am only waiting." He died a short time after, and said to his wife, "I shall die to-day, send my friends word, but send 'Lidgett,' of Lincoln a telegram, 'I have gone home.'" I received the telegram at four o'clock, he died at half-past two.

My life has been full for the last ten years of these experiences.

T. L. LIDGETT'S TRIP TO SWITZERLAND.

On the 6th June, 1906, I left Lincoln about 1 o'clock by the Great Central Railway to Hull, and left there by steamer "Duke of Clarence" for Ze Brugge at 6 p.m., and as my wife and son were with me I shall say "we" in some parts of this trip. The "Duke of Clarence" is a splendid twin-screw steamer belonging to the Lancashire and Yorkshire Railway Co. We had a splendid passage out. I got up next morning about 4.30, and went into the stoke hold, pulled my jacket off and helped to feed the fires with coal. After that I had my breakfast, and spent the remainder of the time on deck looking for the Belgian shore, where we arrived at 7.50 a.m.

on June 7th. We then got in the express for Brussels, arrived before 10 o'clock, and spent the day looking round the city, and left at 6.20 p.m. by the express for Basle in Switzerland, arrived at 5.50 a.m. on June 8th. We were now in Switzerland expecting to see some pretty sights. We left Basle a little after 7 o'clock for the district of the Jura, where we spent several pleasant days doing business and seeing friends. On Sunday, June 10th, the town band where we were staying was playing in the street at 5 a.m., and at 8 there was a bicycle race and hundreds of people. At 9.45 we went to church, but did not know a word that was said; we left church at 11, then the business shops were open for trade—a change that I had never had before on the Sabbath day. We left the Jura district on June 13th for Lucerne, arrived at 7.40 p.m., on the 14th we had a trip on the lake in a steamer, on the 15th we went in a steamboat to Fluelen and Brunnen, on the 16th to Zurich, and up the Rigi in the evening, and looked down on the clouds below us, on Sunday—a rest day. On Monday morning we left Lucerne by train at 5.20 a.m. for the St. Gotthard tunnel, arrived 8.25, went to Andermatt in a carriage, then through the St. Gotthard tunnel at 12.30 for Lugano, arrived at 3.10. In the evening we went up Mount San Salvatore and down at 8 p.m., left Lugano on June 19th for Milan Exhibition in Italy at 6.30 a.m., back to Lugano 7.20 p.m. We left Lugano for Pallanza in Italy by steamer on June 20th at 8.40 a.m., arrived at 12.20. In the afternoon we went to two islands where oranges, lemons, and figs were growing. The names of the islands are Isola Bella and Isola Madre, and on June 21st we left Pallanza at 10.15 a.m., arrived at Baveno 10.25, left at 12.38 to go through the Simplon tunnel, twelve and a half miles through, and arrived at Montreux at 6 p.m., left Montreux 7.11 a.m., June 22nd for Geneva in a steamer 60 miles on Lake Geneva, arrived 10.25, left at 1 p.m. for the north again, arrived at 6 p.m., left here on June 23rd for a village called Les Brenets at 11.10 a.m., arrived there at 12.50. We went for a row on the river on the French frontier, saw two or three eagles, and had a pleasant day. Sunday June 24th, had a thorough rest. After leaving Les Brenets we called at several towns, doing business and looking round the pretty places. In the evening of the same day we went up a mountain, and about 7.30. p.m. we could plainly see Mount Blanc 100 miles away, the setting sun having a very beautiful effect on the snow with which it was covered. On June 26th, we went for a 30 miles drive arriving back at our destination at 7 p.m. On June 27th, my son and his friends climbed up the highest point of the Jura range of mountains, 6,000 feet high, where a lovely view was obtained. This was too much for us old folks, so we stayed down in the village. We left Switzerland at 11.30 p.m. on June 27th, arrived at Brussels 8.18 a.m. June 28th, changed trains to Bruges, arrived at 10 o'clock, spent the day looking round, then went to the steamer "Duke of Clarence," left at 5 p.m. eight miles along the canal for Ze Brugge, left for Hull at 7 p.m. The sea was as smooth as glass when we left Ze Brugge, but it came on rough about 11 p.m., I was up at 4.30 a.m., very ill, and was going to the firemen but could not bear the heat and the smell of the engines, so stayed on deck looking for the first sight of England, and the clump of trees on Driby Hill top, a few miles out of Alford, was the first glimpse I had of home, then the Gossebaugh at Donna Nook near North Somercotes, Spurn Point and Grimsby Tower were the next, arrived at Hull 8 a.m., Lincoln 11.45 a.m. on Friday, June 29th.

We were well treated by the Swiss people. They don't live on luxurious food, chiefly milk, coffee, bread, butter, cheese, jam, honey. They are so polite in their manners, they nearly made a polite man of me, but I dropped back in the old rut when I got into Lincolnshire again. The railway porters wear blue loose slops, the postmen, holland, and the watchmakers, grey. Their chief beverage is red and white wine, which they drink like the English do ale. There are thousands of acres of grapes. I saw no wheat, a little barley and oats, and rye. The mountains are from three to fourteen thousand feet high with very rich meadows in the valleys. The water falls from tremendous heights, and the scenery lovely, with the Alps in view with thousands of tons of ice and snow on them.

I conclude with these few verses in rhyme.

Yours ever the same,

T. L. LIDGETT.

THE LIFE OF THOMAS L. LIDGETT.

I LOVE TO HEAR THE ENGINE HUM.

I love to hear the engine hum,
  Likewise the ocean roar;
I love to see the setting sun
  In the western sky once more.
I love to see the birds and trees,
  And the pretty flowers bloom,
When Lincoln Minster I can see
  I'm not very far from home.

I love to hear the reaper sing,
  Binding up the sheaves;
I love to hear the Autumn winds
  Whistling among the leaves.
I love to view the orchards full,
  Not far from the kitchen door;
And when the weather's cold and dull,
  There's a dumpling for the poor.

Now all you men and women hear
  The words I next will say:
To a better country try to steer,
  And don't forget to pray;
And may I meet you one and all
  When time on earth's no more,
Likewise your children great and small,
  On that bright and sandless shore.

T. L. LIDGETT, 201, High Street, Lincoln.

Since I was converted I have always been eager to see old men backsliders and other old sinners saved, and I have the same feeling to-day; we are apt to go a step above them and think they are nothing, when they are of great value these old sinners.

I have had many hardships to meet with in markets, village greens, public houses, and club rooms, where I have done business, but one of the greatest blessings God has ever done for me, was to take the fear of man away. I still keep urging people to pray, that is my great aim, while I live in this world. I have never been ashamed to own Him any-where. My aim is to help people up, and not to put them lower than they are.

My success and power is got in the early morning from four to six o'clock, when my body is rested, my brain clear, alone in my house, then I have sounder judgment, better thoughts, and get the power in secret. Another part of my success is, I don't think myself above the poorest man in the world, I let him feel I am his brother, I tell him I love him.

When I give a "Temperance Address," I don't call the publican and his wife and children and the house, I get in secret and pray for that publican, which does more than all the slander you can say about him. I find many publicans are goodly disposed men. I talk at their table about the Saviour, and they all want to go to Heaven, and lots of them have been brought up in a Sunday School, and were once members of a society, and it is my place as a converted man, to help them back to the road that leads to the Celestial City, and by God's help I have made up my mind to continue in His work as long as I can talk; then die in his favour and go to receive my reward.

I am not a great believer in sect, for I think at the last day he will know his own. I go in my own way, led by the spirit, and I do my duty the best way I can.

I go among Primitives, Wesleyans, Baptists, Salvation Army or anywhere I am asked, and I have always plenty of work, without asking for it. Gold is not everything to me, the Blood of Christ to me is more than all the gold. I know the longest life on earth is a short one, but Eternity lasts for ever. I try to please the people, but several are offended with me, some even have said very hard words about me, but through the power given to me by God himself, I am able to stand to this day. Fifteen shillings a week and the blessing of God with it, is better than thirty shillings in the service of the Devil.

READY MONEY.

"Cash down" is the best term I know, you are in a better position to buy, you can sell for less profit, be happy outside business hours. The men who fail often say at their examination, "trusting people did it," and they have to start business afresh when their hair is grey, through book debts. Many people leave the district when they have got all the credit they can, and leaves their debts unpaid.

Tradesmen have told me that lots of customers owe them a three years' bill, which is unpaid yet. It keeps people back in spiritual matters, it causes men to lie, and helps to make their power very small. It makes people shy at a mission meeting when they owe money, they cannot kneel down to pray; it encourages people to turn from honesty to wretchedness, it piles sin on the top of sin, until life is unbearable, and if I did these things in my trade, I should at once consider myself equally as bad as the one who didn't pay.

I know tradespeople who always push their trade, whether their goods are paid for or not, and have heard them say, "It doesn't matter." I think they bring their own curse on themselves. If I cannot live at my trade, cash down, I cannot on credit.

An article I sell at thirty-two shillings, my customers tell me they pay sixty-four shillings if they pay weekly for the same sort of article, that means making the poor to be poorer, tempting them to get lower and lower.

When the young men marry, many go to a weekly shop and they are poor all their lives, the beginning has no good foundation.

Money isn't everything to me, but it is one of the greatest blessings in any home when it is rightly used. Lovers of gold hate to part with it when they have it in their pocket and they owe it. The diligent man in business who puts his trust in the Lord and gives good value for good money is the happiest tradesman I know.

I know some of the poorest men in Lincoln and through the country who have but little money and are the best Christians I know. If a man's mind be bent on money it eats his heart away like a "wasp eating a ripe pear."

I once heard of a fireman on a railway engine who had twenty-four shillings a week, and a good Christian man; but when he got promoted to be a driver and had forty-five shillings a week, he lost his religion in a year.

MORALS.

I know people who have got prosperous, who spend much money in drink, cigars and all kinds of pleasure; but the man who has none to spare, stops at home and reads his Bible.

I have been amongst all conditions of men for many years, but when a man is blest with money and a thankful heart, it is well with him. But I have also learnt the poor man can have everlasting life without money, and that is one of the things I glory in. "Heaven is not bought with gold; but he that believeth on the Son, hath life."

I have also been amongst our churches and chapels, it appears as though it was a "devil's playground" to get among members and get them to hate one another and cause ill feeling, and part with their religion and be lost. The best way I know is to live day by day, put your trust in no man; but trust in the Lord, and it shall be well with thy soul.

I wish the people of our churches would love one another more, we should have a better country to live in, in a very short time; but when some want to be first and are not, cause an uproar, dissatisfied, and leave the church. I am glad to know that any man can pray in secret and be blessed, if he has slipped astray, can return without going to the penitent form.

CLEARER MIND.

What pays me best to-day is, if possible to get to bed early say 9 o'clock, up at 4.30 a.m., when the body has had seven hours sleep, I am then ready for getting up. There is no bed-pulling with me since I have been an abstainer from intoxicating drinks and tobacco. I am ready for an early breakfast, my judgment is better, mind clearer, and I can plan my business, and then go and get it done, while I should only be thinking about it if my system was saturated with drink and tobacco essence.

My appetite is good, I can digest well the food that is suitable for good health, if I nourish the body with good wholesome food, it is better for the soul.

The ways of some years of my life were quite different, if I had a whiskey and cigar supper I was not half as fit for having a prosperous day in trade, so by God's help I am going to have no more beer or tobacco while I live. We cannot behave too well to ourselves, work well, sleep well, eat well and doing right in our transactions gives more nerve power than all the excitement in sinful pleasure, which is sure to bring a great amount of grief and pain in our later years.

I advise all young people to try the above methods from sixteen to sixty years of age. It will pay them well.

TEMPERANCE.

In the ordinary way teetotallers sign a pledge book and begin to call the publicans; but I feel in my own heart I am a friend to the publicans; they are put down by a good many teetotallers as the worst lot of men on earth, but I speak as I have experienced, they are ordinary men, and not many of them like drunkenness in their house. They are watched closer than ordinary men are, they do not hawk drink in the streets, they don't put it outside their windows, one must go into the trap before he is trapped; and if a public house is a trap to tempt men to sin, keep outside.

We are not obliged to sin, because we live in a sinful world, there is a power in Christ that has kept me about 12 years from intoxicating drinks, and that power is the same to-day as ever, and there is no keeping powers like it.

It is no wonder the unconverted sneer and laugh at religion when so many of our leading men of Churches and Chapels play with this deadly weapon of soul's destruction.

Some of our teetotallers are the meanest men to do trade with, they appear by their ways that they want nobody to live but themselves; they are not all so.

If a man is a teetotaller and sets a good example to his family, his neighbour, and the world, I call him a good fellow, but if he is a teetotaler because he is too mean to spend three half-pence, I would not give much for a thousand of them, they bring no glory to God or themselves.

If teetotallers were to build Temperance Hotels and plenty of good stabling, they would be fighting against sending the farmers and other persons who come to our markets and other places on business, to public houses for their food and stabling for their horses; but in my way of looking at things, we are keener of building mock theatres to make money, than working for the salvation of souls. I know a good many will be offended with this short story, but I don't mind who is, and who is not.

THE TOBACCO SMOKING CHRISTIAN.

LAST NIGHT OF THE YEAR, 1903.

A few more hours and the year will be gone for ever. I was once a Tobacco Smoker, and often spent from four to five shillings a week on this indulgence; but when I was converted the quickening power of the Holy Spirit, after five minutes on my knees before God, took away the desire for it. What I have seen since that day among Christians is almost heart-breaking. It is a habit of a most filthy and offensive nature. I know men and women and boys who by habitual indulgence have rendered themselves an offence to all clean and decent people. I have spoken to leading Ministers of the Gospel, to Class Leaders and Sunday School Teachers whose breath has been so foul that I have been glad to get away from them.

I can easily excuse this habit in unconverted men, but when followers of Christ and leaders of people in the good way to Heaven indulge in it, puffing their good money away in smoke, and at the same time beseeching those outside their Churches and Chapels to help them to free their buildings from debt. I am astounded, and wonder if before commencing their begging expedition if they have dared to lay the matter before God and to seek His direction. For I am convinced that if enquiry be made in secret before God, the pipe and tobacco will cease with that person. I know and love local preachers who work for the bread that perishes six days in the week and on the seventh travel many miles to publish the good news of a Saviour's love. I also know the man behind the counter who is also a Christian who sells to men 2/- worth of tobacco in the week. Now if this money was spent in their home how much brighter the home would be. Or if it were devoted to the reduction of Chapel debts or to Christian work of some kind, these buildings would soon be free and the Lord's work in the world would advance by leaps and bounds.

THE LIFE OF THOMAS L. LIDGETT.

The contrast between 2/- per week in a filthy indulgence and a penny per week for God's cause wants considering, and if considered well a different course would soon be taken. Brother, pray about it. If it be beneficial to a Christian man to smoke, then surely Christian women and boys and girls have all the same right to indulge in it. I hope all smoking Christians will ask themselves a few questions in God's presence concerning the habit:—Does it make me a nobler looking man, a better husband or father? Does it make me appear more heavenly or does it disgrace me in the sight of God? Can I with greater efficiency lead a class of Christian men and women? Can I more effectively teach a class of children? Can I, because of this habit, discharge any Christian duty with better results? If not, then as a Christian who wants to make most of himself for God and for men, I must give it up at once.

I have sometimes seen persons calling themselves men, enter a non-smoking compartment in a train and ask a shy retiring girl if she objects to smoking, and taking silence for consent have proceeded to annoy every non-smoking person present, by compelling them to inhale the filthy smoke from a pipe that has not been cleansed for many a month.

Dear Christian brother, let us lead others along paths that are safe. The unconverted are crying out against us about the example we set before them. May God baptize us with the Holy Ghost, that we may present to the world a life that is clean, and to copy which will mean purity and power on earth, and glory in the life to come.

Yours,

T. L. LIDGETT.

TO THE DRINKING CHRISTIAN.

The evil of drink is known to every observer. You all know the slaughter it has made during the past year. It has cost the country in money £190,000,000. If we want the country we live in to be a sober country, then it is the duty of the converted to lead the way, but as long as Teetotallers put money in breweries and Christians drink intoxicating

MORALS.

liquors I do not see how we are to prosper, and in the work of Converting Sinners we are practically useless.

When, on the morning of September 29th, 1896, I besought the Lord in mighty faith, He gave me power to say that I would have no more intoxicating drink, and since that day the power has been continually renewed greatly to my advantage in every way. But I go to places where Local Preachers and other Church Officials are seen in alehouses at 10 o'clock on Saturday night, and on Sunday they have to hold services and engage in various kinds of Christian work. Dear brothers, this is tampering with God's mercy to us. Let us avoid it, let us never taste that which destroys both body and soul of both parents and children. Let us never play with such an agent of destruction. The lover of drink says for his excuse that Christ made wine for the wedding. But no one can prove that the wine He made was of the intoxicating sort which bewilders the brain he has given to man. And if Christ did not make intoxicating drink then or at any other time, then I take it that its home and origin is hell; and as none of us want to go there, let us leave off or avoid that which carries men there in such fearful numbers.

I know people who say with good reason that if it were not for the public house, home would be a little heaven. The publican only gets what is taken to him, and the man who takes his money to him instead of using it in the purchase of home comforts cannot get rid of his responsibility and put it on the publican's shoulders. Let us pray for the publican as well as for his victim and prayer for both will prevail.

The old year 1903 will be past in four hours. May God give me more power day by day, that the coming year may be a happy one with us all.

God bless us all, evermore,

T. L. LIDGETT.

Orchard House, Spring Hill, Lincoln.

One beautiful morning in 1899, I walked into a village churchyard in Lincolnshire and read the names of several people whom I had known years gone by. The gravestones stood erect as an emblem of the departed who lay quietly at rest till the trumpet shall sound that will awake them; but there they lay, undisturbed by either a hot summer's sun or the winter's cold blast. The whistling wind among the trees, the rumbling of the trains going by, the clattering of the horses hoofs on the highway, the bleating of the sheep in the fields or the singing of the birds in the branches were all unheard by them. I stood and mused, and remembered that I and all the people now living would in a few short years be numbered with these sleepers of the dust. Men who I have talked to, laughed with, sold my goods to, are already there, reader, we shall soon be among that number. How does this concern you? When your coffin is lowered into the earth by the grave-digger and an assistant, will your soul be lost in hell or will it be in that City which needs no light of the sun but the Lamb of God is the light thereof, may you and I have our sins washed away in the blood of Jesus, and meet around His throne in glory and praise Him to all eternity is the heart's desire of your friend.

T. L. LIDGETT.

A FEW WORDS TO THE NEW BEGINNERS IN BUSINESS.

Never commence trade with high notions and an empty pocket, it is better to have a basket and hawk goods from door to door, than cut a show on borrowed money. Do not think you are better than other people, if God has prospered you, keep humble and very thankful day by day, it will give you more spirit to work and when you have earned one pound, it is yours, take care of it. When you are sixty years old, your hair grey, teeth gone, back up, and you begin to trail your feet when you walk; it is very pleasant to yourself to have a few pounds to help you in your old age.

Keep from spending time and money in a dram shop, pull your jacket off and work, and "Thou shalt be blessed by the labour of thine own hands," so the Bible says, and I believe it. Amen.

I have been connected with Primitive Methodists since I was converted, but I don't glory in being a Primitive, "Let not the wise man glory in his wisdom, neither let the mighty

MORALS.

man glory in his might. Let not the rich man glory in his riches, but let him that glorieth, glory in that which he understandeth and knoweth that Christ is the Lord."

I am sorry to say that in my experience I have found as much enmity in a lot of chapels as there is in a public house. I have known, to my heart's sorrow, men in a public house drink and fight, then have a drink and shake hands and be friends again in a very short time. I have also known men disagree about chapel work, and be years before they are friends.

I wish all the leading ministers, local preachers, school teachers, and class leaders, would never touch drink or tobacco, the unconverted are laughing at them, and I know boys are talking about them. It is very delightful to hear a short address from the pulpit on a Sunday morning to the children, but the man who touches these things himself, and the children know it, has very little power with the children.

If we all want to go to the same heaven, why not be brothers here. If we have a dinner, or a shilling to give, give it to some one in need and not always those that have plenty in their own cupboards, and what you give, do it in secret, and "the Lord will reward you openly, His word declares it."

MY EXPERIENCE IN "WATCH" SELLING.

In my opinion I have just been the man to please the people in selling them a good watch for a little money, and when I have sold a watch it is mine no longer, the property belongs to someone else, but when it is broken they blame me and want it repairing for nothing. A watch does not break in an ordinary way, by wearing, it is either by accident or bad usage. I have known men and women preach a long yarn about a broken watch and when I have asked them how they have got to know these things and not learnt the trade, they can prove nothing, it is to get out of paying for the damage they have done to the watch. I have hundreds of another kind of customer, men and women who are not reckless with their watches, they take care of them, and when they have worn them several years, they are in better condition

(43)

than some watches are that have been worn a year. A man that is not careful with his watch. it very often happens, is careless in most things. Let us all live daily on the watch tower, that we may be in a safe place at the last day.

ON THE SO-CALLED EASY PAYMENT SYSTEM.

A great many people like to be trusted with goods unpaid, but I have not found many of this class want to pay at all, they will tell lies, lock the door if they know the collector is coming round. If you give some credit and they go past your shop, they are very often busily engaged looking across the street, until they have got past, their manliness seems to have quite left them, it makes them cease from praying in a meeting, from exhorting sinners to come to Christ in the street, and causes many to turn into a by-lane and leave walking in the middle of the king's highway. These people I am not seeking to trade with. I find there are a lot of people with both eyes wide open to spend their money to the best advantage and I do trade with a great quantity of this kind. I had a person ask me the price of an article, it was £2 (two pounds), and the person said, "I paid three guineas for one like it, on the weekly game." If you call this easy payment, you see it very different to me, I call it a very hard way through life of your own making. Take a lesson from the birds, before they hatch their young, they prepare their nest first. Young men and women do the same, then you will only have to pay twenty shillings to the £1 (one pound), instead of thirty. What ready money has done for me often makes my heart glow with gladness. It also makes you bold without whiskey, happy when you live without being excited with wine. A better home, a horse and trap to ride in.

I am sixty three years of age, and go to sell in markets and in villages until 10 o'clock at night, and I am well blest by the labour of my body.

I hope someone will be benefited by this short epistle.

Good night.

MORALS.

A FEW REMINDERS OF THE PAST.

On the morning of the great gale, May 28th, 1860, I had been in "farmers' service" a few days, when I got an order from my master the night before to walk to his son's, four or five miles across the country. It blew and rained so hard, I was nearly exhausted when I got there, and I was so cold and wet, I was told to go against the fire to dry my clothes. After I had been there about an hour I went to help another man to clean a bullock shed out, the door was propped open with a piece of wood and the wind blew the wood away, just before I entered the shed, and the door knocked me down into a large hole full of water, I was wet through to the skin and remained so. Thousands of trees were blown up by the roots that day.

Christmas eve of the same year was the coldest day and night I have ever known in my life. I have heard many men say the same, and also that night has been mentioned in our "Lincolnshire Chronicle," more than once.

A few places I have visited, the "Field of Waterloo," where the battle was fought in 1815. I have also visited Hamburg, in Germany, about 400 miles across the North Sea from Grimsby, in the Great Central Steamer "Lutterworth," and came back in the "Nottingham."

I have also been to Scotland a few times. The greatest distance I have been to sell watches is Motherwell, Hamilton and Dundee. I have spent a few days in the Isle of Man.

THE SABBATH DAY.

About 12 years ago I was selling in the Temperance Hall, Retford. I read the 58th Chapter of Isaiah, and the last two verses brought me to a conclusion that I would never enter a train, or horse and trap on the Sabbath day, and up to now I have kept that up.

As an unconverted young man I went to Grimsby in 1864, and one Sunday morning I went out of my lodgings for a walk before breakfast, and in my morning's walk I went to a mill that was on fire. I had on the same suit as you read about in the fore part of my history (when I went out to sea). I got my clothes very dirty with working at this fire all Sunday and got three shillings and two glasses of beer, and I have not worked on the Sabbath day since. Praise the Lord for leading me as He has done. I read the Sabbath is a day of rest, but in a good many cases it is a hard day. Some women are busy baking and doing house work most of the time, while hundreds of men are idling about, looking at pigs in the stye, and judging each others' gardens (namely) Sunday farming, then go out with a party in the afternoon in a waggonette, or by train for an outing.

If I wanted to go to Market Rasen, fifteen miles, any day in the week to sell a watch, the fare would be two shillings and sixpence, except Tuesday, market day, which would then be two shillings, but on Sunday the railway company throws out the tempting bait. You can go for sixpence, a scandalous thing for a Sabbath day, it does not pay in the long run. I should like to see the railways belong to the state, there would be cheaper rates for the people to pay for their outing, and not all grab for a great dividend to the shareholders of this country.

When I see ladies and gentlemen in motor cars on the Sabbath day, and they stop for anything, I just look at their faces, there is not a happy face scarcely amongst them, and there are not many happy people who are continually breaking the Sabbath day. I wish we could very speedily see the Sunday without the clatter of horses hoofs, or the rumbling trains and the flying motor cars, and going so far on a bicycle to get drink, or the river fisherman, with his basket and line.

This is not written for argument with me, when we meet. Please argue it out with your own conscience.

I commenced to write this at 3-30 a.m., Monday, June 1st, 1908.

As near as I can remember, it was in the year 1894, I was selling at the Temperance Hall, Retford, before I was converted, I read the 58th chapter of Isaiah, and the last two verses struck me with great force that the Lord would bless me more if I would honour the Sabbath, which reads as follows:—"If thou turn away thy foot from the Sabbath, from doing thy pleasure on My holy day; and call the Sabbath a delight, the holy of the Lord, honourable; and shalt honour Him, not doing thine own ways, nor finding thine own pleasure, nor speaking *thine own* words: Then

MORALS.

shalt thou delight thyself in the Lord; and I will cause thee
to ride upon the high places of the earth and feed thee with
the heritage of Jacob thy father: for the mouth of the Lord
hath spoken *it*."

So I wrote home and told my wife I should never come
home on a Sunday again, and from that day to now I have
never ridden in a train or trap on the Sabbath day. PRAISE
THE LORD for giving me the power to resist the temptations
which are thrown out by Railway Companies to Sabbath
breakers. People of Lincoln who know part of my career
can see for themselves how the Lord has blessed me. Home is
a splendid place on the Sabbath, when a man has toiled all
the week. If men would drink less intoxicants and smoke less
tobacco and get wisdom, we should not have men with fishing
baskets and other ways of making Sunday a hard day, and on
Monday morning more tired than when they gave over work
on Saturday. Brothers and sisters, consider these things.
The man or woman that takes the Bible for their lawyer are
seldom at a lawyer's office seeking advice and paying 6s. 8d.
for it.

God bless and help all readers of this leaflet. And may
we seek and also find that WONDER WORKING POWER, *the Holy
Ghost*, which cleanses from all sin and makes us fit for the
Kingdom of Heaven.

May I meet you there through the blood of the cross.

Your friend,

T. L. LIDGETT,

Orchard House, Spring Hill, Lincoln.

Here are a few favourite verses of mine, sent to me after
the death of a very great friend of mine in 1890.

THE WATER MILL.

Listen to the water mill through the livelong day,
How the clicking of its wheel wears the hours away.
Languidly the Autumn winds stir the greenwood leaves;
From the fields the reapers sing binding up the sheaves;

THE LIFE OF THOMAS L. LIDGETT.

And a proverb haunts my mind, as a spell is cast,
The mill will never grind with the water that has passed.

Autumn winds revive no more, leaves that once are shed;
And the sickle cannot reap corn once gathered;
   And the rippling stream flows on, tranquil, deep, and still
   Never gliding back again to the water mill.
Truly speaks the proverb old, with a meaning vast,
The mill will never grind with the water that has passed.

Take the lesson to thyself, loving heart and true,
Golden years are fleeting by, youth is passing too;
   Learn to make the most of life, lose no happy day,
   Time will never bring thee back chances swept away;
Leave no tender word unsaid, love while love shall last,
The mill will never grind with the water that has passed.

Work while yet the daylight shines, man of strength and will,
Never does the streamlet glide useless by the mill;
   Wait not till to-morrow's sun beams upon the way,
   All that thou canst call thine own lies with thee to-day,
Power, intellect and health may not always last,
The mill will never grind with the water that has passed.

Oh the wasted hours of life, that have drifted by!
Oh, the good we might have done lost without a sigh!
   Love that we might once have saved by a single word,
   Thoughts conceived, but never penned, perishing unheard
Take the proverb to thine heart, take and hold it fast,
The mill will never grind with the water that has passed.

Oh! love thy God and fellow man, thyself consider last,
For come it will, when thou must scan dark errors of the past;
   And when the fight of life is o'er, and earth recedes from
                                view,
   And heaven in all its glory shines, midst the pure, the
                            good, the true,
Then you'll see more clearly, the proverb deep and vast,
The mill will never grind with the water that has passed.

MORALS,

TO THE UNSAVED.

My dear Friends,

I write this to you at six o'clock on the morning of the 10th of July, 1908, and I pray that God will lead me to write something that will be helpful. Some of you are not accustomed to go to either Church or Chapel, so I have sent this message to you that Christ says "Come unto Me and be ye saved."

I was leaving a public house one cold winter's morning to walk a mile and half to a Railway Station, when a friend put his hand on my shoulder and gave me a few words of encouragement of the Saviour's love to sinners, and when he had left me about five minutes I was converted, on a railway bridge, so you see I had not to go to Church or Chapel to be saved, I was alone with Christ my Saviour, I saw and felt my need of Him and found Him and I was no better than the worst of you, so I invite you to come, and if you come conditionally, to give up all sin He will forgive all the past, and receive you into His family, but don't be misled as many want the good feeling before they believe, take God at His word, believe now—He saves you, and the peace of God which passeth all understanding will fill your hearts. God help and save you all from the wrath to come. If you cannot see your way clear to the Cross, and you see me in the street or market ask me and I will do my best to help you.

God bless you all for ever,

T. L. LIDGETT.

MY MODE OF LIVING.

I eat nothing only what is good, such as bread and butter, dry toast and fat bacon, boiled fish occasionally, good vegetables and short pudding.

I put two ozs. of Epsom Salts to a quart of boiling water and take a wine-glass full every morning all the year round. Our ailments would be very few if we all did this.

D

THE LIFE OF THOMAS L. LIDGETT.

I go to bed at nine or before and am up again at four, that is the way, if you mean to have a good day.

This book is not written for an advertisement, but to help and encourage people to be sober, thrifty and good.

I have had it printed as I talk, not grammatical or to appear a fine fellow.

God bless us all for ever, and I pray that I may meet you all in Heaven.

MY CHARACTER AND MY FRIEND.

How often I've longed for a trustworthy friend,
  On whom in all seasons my heart might depend,
Both my joy and my sorrow to share;
  But I met with so much disappointment and pain,
That I feared all my seeking would prove to be vain,
  So I nearly gave o'er in despair.

I was friendless and sad, my heart burdened with grief,
  And I knew not to whom I could look for relief,
When I heard a voice so gentle and calm;
  Oh come unto me lay thy head on my breast
And I will refresh thee, in me find thy rest,
  And I'll ever protect thee from harm.

I will sooth thee in sorrow, will comfort in pain,
  You will never seek my assistance in vain,
Then refuse not my offer of love;
  I will heighten thy joy, I will lessen thy woe,
I will guide thee through life in the path thou should go,
  And will safely convey thee above.

I listened with pleasure so sweet was the voice,
  So soothing the tone I could not but rejoice,
For I felt that his sayings were true;
  And now I well know that he used no deceit,
For I'm sure that the hours that I've spent at his feet
  Are the happiest ever I knew.

MY CHARACTER AND MY FRIEND.

He stilleth my passions, he calmeth my fears,
  He changeth the aspect of death as it nears,
And bids me confide in his love;
  He whispers his infinite power to save,
To snatch me at last from the realms of the grave,
  To dwell in his presence above.

In what words can I speak of the worth of my friend,
  Having loved me once he will love to the end,
Though I oftimes forgetful may be;
  Every cause of estrangement I would humbly defy,
So deep and so long, so broad and so high,
  Is the love that he beareth to me.

And how can I tell of the deeds he hath done,
  Of the manner in which my affection he won,
Of his goodness, his kindness, his grace;
  I was lost, and he found me: I was blind, he gave sight,
My path was a dark one but he made it light,
  And brightened the gloomiest place.

I was filthy and foul, but he made me quite clean,
  And covered with rags for a long time I'd been,
But he gave me a garment to wear;
  'Twas a beautiful robe, no defect could I see,,
For he made it himself and then gave it to me,
  That I might look lovely and fair.

I had broken the law, I was sentenced to die,
  I knew I was guilty had naught to reply
And my conscience tormented me sore;
  When my friend came in view, showed his hands and his side
And told me that once in my stead he had died,
  That I might have life evermore.

Such then is my friend, oh I wish I could sound
  The praise of his name to earth's uttermost bound,
I would sound it again and again;
  Do you ask who it is that has stilled my complaints?
Oh listen ye sinners, oh praise Him ye Saints,
  It is Jesus, the Saviour of men.

T. L. LIDGETT, LINCOLN.

(51)

LOSS OF THE "LONDON."

(This ship was lost in 1866).

'Twas on the sixth morn of the year,
  Long ere the break of day,
The " London," for Australia's shore,
  Steamed out of Plymouth bay.

As o'er the breezy Channel's waves
  The good ship swiftly bore,
How many, many weeping eyes
  Looked back on England's shore?

Ay! and how many weeping ones
  Gazed from the English strand,
And saw, with tears, and hopes, and fears,
  The "London" leave the land?

How many prayers were prayed that day
  Upon the land and sea?
"God comfort those we leave behind,
  And with them ever be.

God comfort those who part from us,
  To cross the ocean wide—
Thou, strong to save, on land or wave,
  Be ever at their side."

The land fades out, the sun has left
  The boding western sky,
A moaning wind creeps o'er the waves,
  And loud the sea-birds cry.

The captain stood beside the wheel,
  Proud of his ship was he;
He looked up to the dark'ning sky,
  He looked along the sea.

" 'Tis as I thought—'twill come to blow
  Before the break of day—
And let it come, and welcome, too,
  'Twill give my good ship way."

LOSS OF THE LONDON.

The morning dawned in gloom and rain,
  The waves tossed wild and far,
The wind came down in angry gusts,
  And shook each mast and spar.

And there was doubt on many a lip,
  And fear in many an eye,
As the big waves broke, and swept like hail
  Across the topmast high.

But when they saw their captain's eyes,
  Where terror ne'er yet shone,
And when they heard his hopeful word,
  Their doubt and fear were gone.

Still on, still on through lashing rain,
  On, through the driving spray,
While the wind shrieked loud, in sheet and shroud,
  The good ship held her way.

Another day dawned dull and gray,
  And wilder blew the gale,
Blast after blast, till down went mast,
  And spar, and shroud, and sail.

Heavily, heavily rose the ship
  Upon the raging swell,
And heavily, heavily in the trough
  Of the mountain waves she fell.

And the wind still blew, and the gale still grew,
  Till came the hurricane!
Ah! in that hour of stormy power,
  The might of man was vain.

But strong as is the hurricane,
  And terrible the sea,
Yet is there ONE whose words once stilled
  The waves of Galilee,

And unto Him, prayer after prayer
  Was rising night and day,
While slowly through the storm-beat sea
  The "London" held her way.

And many took the Blessed Book,
  And turned its pages o'er,
And found the words of peace and love,
  And life for evermore.

Next morn the captain strode the deck
  With wan and weary gaze—
Brave man, he had not closed an eye
  For four long nights and days.

He looked upon the driving clouds,
  Along the waves looked he,
"I've weathered many a storm, but one
  Like this I ne'er did see."

Then rose a servant of the Lord,
  A preacher true and brave,
And cried to Him, who rides the storm,
  And calms the troubled wave.

"God grant that all on board this day,
  Amid this stormy sea,
May raise their love to heaven above,
  And turn their hearts to Thee."

With deep'ning night, in giant might,
  Down came the awful storm,
And on the swell, uprose and fell
  The "London's" battered form.

Then, in an hour that might appal
  The bravest man of men,
The captain shouted, "Turn her head
  To Plymouth once again!"

LOSS OF THE LONDON.

'Twas done, alas! 'twas done in vain,
  For, ere the close of day,
The good ship settled down and sank
  In Biscay's stormy bay.

Oh! let us hope, while to her doom
  The fated ship was driven,
Each life's last word and prayer were heard,
  Each sinner was forgiven,

And, when she sank, that every soul
  Was wafted to that shore
Where death-divided friends shall meet,
  And partings are no more.

THE END.

www.ingramcontent.com/pod-product-compliance
Lightning Source LLC
Chambersburg PA
CBHW081525040426

42447CB00013B/3345